Mosaic
_of_ _the_ Dark

Mosaic
of
the **Dark**

poems

Lisa Dordal

Black
Lawrence
Press

www.blacklawrence.com

Executive Editor: Diane Goettel
Book and Cover Design: Amy Freels
Cover Art: "Undersea Landscape" © Jill Samuels

Published 2018 by Black Lawrence Press.
Printed in the United States.

For Laurie

Contents

Commemoration

Commemoration

i. Christmas Pageant

At twelve, I played Mary
in a community Christmas pageant.
I saw you at the service, people said.
I saw you with your baby,
riding your donkey. A real donkey,
led by some boy. Older boy.
Fourteen at least. I don't remember
his name or if I even knew it
at the time. Just that I couldn't look at him.
Couldn't look straight at him
without blushing and lowering my eyes.
Everyone said I made a great Mary.
That I did a great job being
the one God descended upon. No,
not descended upon. Entered.
That I did a great job being the one
God entered. And who
afterwards called it holy.

ii. Christmas Pageant Revisited

The boy is important, the visiting poet said.
Immensely important. The center of the poem,
he said. Her desire for him is the center of the poem,
the *dramatic* center. Her desire for him is
what this poem is about. This much is clear:
She *desires* him. The girl riding a donkey
desires him, the boy, the dramatic center.

You need to build him up more,
he continued. Give him a name, good looks,
maybe a touch of acne. Help us to see him,
to see the real center of this poem.
To see *into* the center; to see inside her
desire. Help us to get inside—
inside the blushing and the lowering.
Tell us how blue his eyes are, how dark his hair,
how straight and perfect his
nose. We need to *see* him. The center
of her desire. Unless, of course, you are striving
(*striving!*) to create an aura of mystery—
an *illusion* of mystery—like you would
if you were talking about, say, God.

For the Cashier at T. R. Wolfe's Toy and Candy

To enter the pinched interior
of T. R. Wolfe's Toy and Candy,

was to risk her squint
that branded every kid

a thief. Her hair pulled back
into a coarse, gray stone,

her face bony and sad—
as we'd tap our fingers

against the counter glass
to pronounce our choice

of pink cigarettes cloaked
in sugary smoke. Or,

from the sundry collection
of jigsaw puzzles lining

the store's high-shelved
perimeter: our choice

of Barbie and Ken's
dream house, the cockpit

of a Concorde, UFOs
over a Midwest wheat farm.

Puzzles that would spread
like sea garbage

across our bedroom floors.
How can it be that this

is what was given her?
Not a pursuit of quiet,

brainy labor: reading the ash
in Nile River mud.

Or probing the loss
of an ancient grave—

head to head, a girl and a boy,
and beads too many

to count. Only this, the daily repetition
of warm coins passing

from our hands into hers.
And how can I not admire her

for her refusal to feign
contentment?

Whatever it was she wanted,
getting us instead.

Elevator Ride with Famous Poet

After my sudden confession of love,
he extends his arm, patting the sleeve of my coat—

Is it raining? he asks—
like a hungry ant tapping on the abdomen

of the one carrying in its mandibles
a soft globe of dew

because doesn't the poet need the world
as much as the world needs

the poet? As a child, I watched my father
lean his body over our Chevy's

black complexity of metal. Watched him
draw out the looped end of the rod,

commanding an entire constellation of knowledge
in a single luminous pull—a language

I was never expected to master, only
to practice over that dense geography

the one small phrase taught
to my tourist body, my tourist mind.

It is raining. It has rained. It will have been
raining. And in the Coral Sea, just east of Australia,

the island that was thought to be,
drawn as it was onto maps, the new

following the old—this repetition of inclusion—
until no one believed it wasn't really there.

It wasn't really there at all. Even a whale
falling to the ocean floor

will be consumed, the tiny organisms feasting,
as if the water itself has teeth. Hungry ant

tapping on the abdomen
of the one carrying a soft globe of dew.

It is raining. It has rained. It will have been
raining.

Holy Week

1. *Intersection*

Your freezer had died—the melted blood of raw,
damp meat, everywhere on the kitchen floor.
Bright and contagious across flat brown tiles.
Father was ten time zones away, studying
the ancient gods of ancient Greece; and we were
stopped at a light two blocks from Sears.
It was there I let form in my mouth
one bated word after another to utter the question—
Have you ever thought you might be...—
that hung in the cramped space between us.
(Father's first words: *Maybe your Mother is, too,*
when I came out.)

It wasn't an option, you said.
Your head never turning, both of us looking straight
into the lucid circle of red that, in that moment,
provided all the direction we cared for.
What more could we say
about a revelation carrying the whole sinewy weight
of non-being. The thousands of ways you'd said no—
deferred, followed, and agreed—making yourself smaller
and smaller, a god of old clay, buried
and powerless. But for the tiny part that broke out,
sneaked out sly: The resounding Yes
of your seventh conception, as if I birthed you.

2. *Holy Week*

Laid up in the heart wing because your valves
weren't right, you couldn't get to your jars
hidden in bookcases throughout the house.

I feel fine, you'd say, every time I called, going on
about the terrible smells and noises and strangers' proddings.
I loved your being there. That whole week,

I loved. That whole week, a clean bright patch
stuck to the stink and slur and soil of every week before.
Several times a day I called, to hear the clearness in

your voice. As if I could store it up somehow, capture it,
go back to it, again and again. To that week,
that one week, when you came back.

3. Recycling

I was sixteen when I found them—still have my notes,
the sheet of lined yellow paper on which I recorded my findings:

four in your sitting room, behind a collector's set
of Hardy Boys mysteries and a neatly ordered run

of *Scientific Americans*. Three smaller ones
in your dresser amidst an assortment of cold crèmes

and sweet perfumes. The largest in your nightstand,
stashed between a stack of *New York Times* bestsellers

and a bookmarked copy of *Good News for Modern Man*.
The jars you didn't use, you'd put in a box

under the kitchen sink until the last Saturday of the month,
when you'd load it into the back of our Chevrolet,

drive to the recycling center and begin (again)—
this time by color—the process of separating.

4. *Visitation*

For three days, I'd kept the windows open,
screen doors latched and breathing,

after your visit. So I was surprised
what little odor there was

arising from your body laid before us.
Cleansed and scentless. Free

of the reeling aura that had clung to you,
lingering in every room you'd ever been

but here.

5. Transaction

After the prayers were spoken,
the hymns sung and your casket closed,

we followed you—Father and I—
through the courtyard blooms

of an early Midwest spring, past
the iron Jesus, blessing without ceasing,

onto the street of too-bright sky,
where the men then turned and passed to Father

your long, silver necklace
(worn always with the dress),

your earrings made of pearl,
and your wedding band; passed,

in the knowing way that men pass tips,
from hand to hand.

6. Passing On

Six years and still I'm finding notes,
like the one taped to the bank where you put funds away for
     extras—
a Mahler record in seventy-two, a wine decanter in eighty-eight.

I received this desk from Sheila, today's note begins,
who bought it from her coworker, Beth McKinley,
who inherited it from Helen Smith, a friend dear to us both.

I found it taped to the underside of your small wooden desk—
mine since Father sold the house, dispersed of things that
     wouldn't fit.
The desk you used as a dressing table,

where you'd darken the edges of your eyes
and make your lips a modest pink.
It is written on a piece of scrap paper—

something about a meeting at church on the back—
and has two rough edges where you folded the paper
to tear it down to size. And tape, brittle and brown

where it stuck to the wood and the wood stuck back.
Until today, when the note fell off during dusting.
Tucked, for years, from view, like the queerness you passed on,

that you received from Ida and she passed on from Lizzie—
passed on until it opened out inside of me,
falling out of hiding.

7. Induction

Of course I asked first. Raised as I was
to be good. *What's one glass?* you said.
At fourteen, surrounded by a spirit
I took for love. Everything hard
softening. The way your own mother
tucked bottles of bourbon
into the folds of your freshly laundered clothes
sent home, during college, for washing.

Two weeks later, my own festive six-pack.
Five brightly sealed bottles on the table,
next to the ornamental angels spinning
round and round from the heat of candles
below. The sixth at my lips: my left fingers
clasping its slender neck, as if it were
a tin whistle. My right hand resting delicately
on the bottle's dark, glassy body. You, next to me,
lovely as ever in your long, green Christmas dress,
hair freshly set, face perfect and bright—
looking straight at me. Smiling. Can you see

why I shuddered when Father's new wife
ordered your drink? "Manhattan"
slipping from her mouth. As though
it was that which he loved, wedded himself to:
the taste on your lips, then hers.
"Manhattan" hovering in the air between us
like some sweet angel of you,
returned.

Matrimonies

Sixth Grade

Under a warm June sun during the break
between Social Studies and Language Arts,

they married us off. Our bodies surrounded
on the cracked pavement of our schoolyard

by friends, classmates, then
by something larger, sovereign and invisible.

Bruce in wide jeans, a pink Oxford button-down,
and brown tie-ups so shiny you could see birds

in the patches of sky they reflected. Everything
about him beautiful. Me, in a short purple dress

and soda-orange sneakers that the older sister
of my best friend told me *had to go.*

A boy named Peter officiated, spoke the words
that blended us together. The same boy

who told me there were two types
of women: that I was the kind men married,

not the kind men used for practicing
(what they never wanted to perfect).

Even in the race-sore seventies
on Chicago's South Side, no one minded

this one rupture, this one tear in the
taut dictates of order: that he was black

and I was white. But they wouldn't tolerate
our queerness. The clang of missed baskets—

other kids shooting hoops—was our music.
That, and the cursing that always followed.

Proposal

In the version we tell,
we're on the train

returning from my parents'.
My left hand in his right,

our backs curving
into the cracking weave

of the seat, train aiming into night:
Ohio, perhaps, or Illinois.

In the version we don't,
we're at their house—

their place of long marriage. Only,
he didn't want them to know

until we were back home.
And my *yes* became a thing

to put away, an ornament
of amber. Together,

we made up the lie. As if
I'd sensed the lie beneath,

figured why not add
another. At twenty-three,

having taken a therapist's advice
to *pretty myself up*. I imagine

my body now, on that train,
after sleep has taken me in:

my hand, limp, separate from his;
my mouth hanging open

in that wide, ridiculous way,
as if my dreams

filled me with dismay.

Wedding

As if the past were present completely
in the laden air of that June day, molded
by the stone walls of the sanctuary,

I walked, as my mother had taught me,
down the aisle, my body
pressed into taut, pallid lace, her own.

Even the tightly folded note my mother
slipped to my bridesmaid to tell her
she was holding her flowers wrong

was a summons from the past
to get things right. And the look I gave
my maid of honor, straight into her eyes

during the spoken vows, was a calling forth,
a calling out. Grandmother, mother,
daughter—there in that moment of keeping

and quiet, quiet breaking. And the Gospel—
slinked in by the preacher—an appeal
to rightnesses of the past, as I said "I do"

with almost every cell and, in the process,
began the long and tight-lipped death
of my mother, who taught me how.

Clues

We were shooting pool in my father's billiard room—
halfway caring about the rules—

when the white ball of Karyn's turn
cracked into a blue, and I heard:

She kissed me! coming out
of Becky's mouth. She on one stool,

me on the other—and there I was,
leaning. This thing my body did, at twelve.

At twenty, I sought out Connie
in the lounge of my dorm, homing in

to get the one small fix my body knew
I needed. She, casually radicalizing

the air around her, pulling a long, sexy drag
on a cigarette, charged words

of Trotsky and Marx splayed across her lap.
Her lips parting for me every time—

a deep-throated "hey" or "hello"
was enough, the way a weekly token

of bread or wine can be enough.
At twenty-nine, the soft grunt of our pastor

(gay and out) when he spied
the Gertrude and Alice poster

in our bedroom. Syllabic m or n to express
confusion, surprise. Or as inquiry

awaiting reply.

Survival

First Memory

I remember the sidewalk.
The way it narrowed, the way

my father, years later, taught me
how to draw a road.

Wider at the bottom, narrower
as I moved up the page, the lines

getting closer and closer,
never meeting. How long it was,

cutting straight down the middle
of their yard, narrowing

as I looked down it towards
the house, towards the stroller.

Never would have happened
if she'd stayed home, people said.

The lines getting closer and closer,
never meeting.

(She, being the mother. It was the seventies.)
I remember the sidewalk.

Not the sound of the phone
that must have rung,

must have been answered.
The lines getting closer and closer.

Not running with my mother
through our yard, through the alley

that separated our yard
from theirs. Me on one edge,

Katherine on the other—both of us
fixed into position.

The sidewalk, not the look
on the housekeeper's face,

not the body, inert, inside
the stroller.

Pretty Moon

Pretty moon, everyone said.
Before the noise, before

the fire. Two cars
and the cornfields idle

on either side. Like the eggs
of monkfish, emerging

a million at a time, knitted
into a gauzy shroud,

forty feet long, buoyant,
built for dispersal—the veil

between us and them,
thin. My cousin,

beautiful at sixteen,
dead at seventeen.

Pretty, pretty moon.
And me, at five, mouth open

not to a scream or even
to a word. Just taking in air,

quietly as a spider
entering a room.

Flash

All those years admiring the photograph—
my father and I dressed for a gathering
of family; dozens of cheery, generic flowers
stitched across the neckline of my shirt; my glasses,
large pink ovals against the perfect skin of my face—
I never saw the fist: twenty-seven tightly clenched bones
flexed playfully in my direction. I look happy.
Which is why I loved the picture for as long as I did.
Pressed it into a book meant for mementos.
My father's right arm embracing me
in the only way that he knew;
his smart blue suit a thing of beauty, reminding us
of the distance he'd come; his beginnings of narrow means,
a fixture in family lore. The way it hung there—
must have hung—in every room my father entered:
compressed regions of tendon storing the energy
he was capable of releasing. My fear
braided into the strands of sinew connecting
good-girl muscle to good-girl bone. As my mother,
with the touch of one finger, let in the tiny light.

Survival

Inside the pizzeria, love's latest news was carved
into the darkly stained surface of every table. The force
of blunt gray knives and shameless teenage muscle
creating a landscape of pique, impeccably done.
Caroline is a bitch. Liz and Tommy forever. Sheila likes pussy.
Later, my own name next to the words "Cock" and "Teaser."
I ordered salad and minestrone—pizza, I knew,
would be messy, one of the many tips I'd read in *Seventeen*
along with: *Look interested. Don't disagree.* And
Be yourself! My date ordered chicken, still on the bone.
There were others after this. Different names;
a father's borrowed cologne filling the air between us.
Eventually, making myself homely, shapeless,
anything to let the "No" come, instead, from them.

35

The Living Room

Lingering in the doorway of the living room,
I studied my father's profile,

the way his jaw jutted out
with its chronic clench of tension.

Even this, I would miss.
He turned briefly to wave his hand,

the goodnight I was sure would be
goodbye. Slowly, then, I walked up

the wide oak stairs, trod raw and plain:
an oval sore, ripe and exposed,

in the center of each step,
then down the narrow hallway

to the back of the house, past
the empty rooms of siblings long moved on.

In the quiet turmoil of my room,
I laid my body down;

took pains to pull the covers up,
tight and close. I had taken such care

not to lose any chalky white residue
to my fingers—the aspirin

I had counted into five tidy rows of ten
before swallowing the pills

one by one. Such care to do this
one thing well. And none of this

will he ever know. *Aspirin?* he'd say.
Aspirin can't kill you.

Testament

On the Way to Emmaus

While they were talking and discussing, Jesus himself came near but their eyes were kept from recognizing him.... One of them, named Cleopas, asked, "Are you the only stranger in Jerusalem who does not know the things that have happened there in these days?"
—Luke 24:14–18

It's easy to see Jesus. We can't
not see him with his thick carpenter arms,
hair the color of Galilee night,
eyes vexed with knowing.
Jesus himself came near.

But you we do not see: the woman,
the wife, the one with Cleopas. You,
the stranger, we do not see, still.

I know what it's like not to be seen;
what it's like to be smoothed over by discourse;
to have the bumpy parts gone,
your own rich texture of being
dulled into round slivers of yearning,
a dark, holy heaviness lost:
the year I taught New Testament—
Paul, the Gospels, Revelation—
and everyone thought I was straight.
You foolish Galatians! I began,
continuing with the offspring
of Christ, the curse of the law,
and the knife that Paul hopes will slip.
Until the last day, when I came out—
one part Christian, one part Jew, all queer.

I know what it's like not to be seen
but, still, my eyes faltered and all I saw
was two men walking, one of whom,
true stranger in the text, was you.

Amanat

On the night of December 16th, 2012, a 23-year-old
physiotherapy student boarded a bus in New Delhi to
return home after watching the film Life of Pi.

The hyena kills the zebra,
then the orangutan.

The tiger kills the hyena.
And the boy survives.

Pi is an irrational number.
And a woman boards a bus.

If horses could draw,
they would draw one god

in the shape of a horse.
Oxen would draw many,

each with a body like their own.
And the bus is not really a bus.

The relationship
between the width of a circle

and its circumference
continues infinitely without

repeating. And Pi is a boy
who just wants to love

God. If dark matter could draw,
it would not draw itself.

The human intestine
is approximately five feet long.

Only five percent of hers
would remain. They would be called

joyriders. The instrument used was
metal. The instrument used

was flesh. And the woman,
it was said, died peacefully.

To Say Something Is Alive Is Not Enough

Because everything is in motion:
bone, ivory, shell. And blood

doesn't hold on to anything
but itself. Because there are worlds

within worlds—geometries
of ant and whale, girl and boy.

And some infinities are larger
than other infinities. Because iron filings

can reveal invisible lines of force.
And my mother's last words were:

help me. Because my father loved
Lincoln's general—the one who drinks

and still wins the War—and the past
is a fine skin that does not protect.

And I did not know that loss could be
so ordinary: my mother reaching

into a cupboard for a glass, saying
take something, anything.

And I don't know if memory
is a place or a map of the place.

Only that I did not come this time
to find her. And I never did ask

what war.

Plumbing the Depths

As he squats by the pedestal of our bathroom sink,
I can see the small metal tab of the plumber's
front-fly zipper, sticking up

like a tiny, totem dick. Like one of those
painted Russian dolls in reverse—
the smallest version, plainly visible,

suggestive of its larger kin. Even the angle,
a perfect match. What every Barbie
was supposed to want in Ken.

And if God is male, then male is God,
which means we come eventually
to the celebrated phallus of the father-god.

"It's not pooling up anymore," I hear the plumber say.
Rarely does a man enter our house
who isn't paid to do so. Electricians, painters—

today a plumber whose name,
I suddenly realize, I never bothered
to find out. But I do know,

that for him, I am "Mrs. Samuels,"
and the husband I don't have is at work,
earning a living for us both.

You Ask How

You ask how and I tell you about the fire,
that day every soft spot lit up

in the deep under-skin of my interior.
My look too long into the eyes I'd loved

since 7th grade. Lips, pinked
and glossed, legs urgently shaved—

the rapidly emerging sex
of our bodies, meant only for boys,

later men. You ask how
and I say: cup tipped on its side,

empty of itself; angel hovering
above her own numb flesh;

walking, until I couldn't tell waking
from sleep. You ask how and I tell you

about the centipedes I had seen
in the night. Reality pressing through

my dream eyes. How I awoke
to find them alive—antennae to tail—

along the white crown molding
of my bedroom. You ask how

and I say: small word forming
in my mouth, in my body,

rising through limb and gut.
The man, the dream. How many times

had I seen this already? The man
to whom I am saying: no.

By morning, only the sticky remains
of a spider's home, sufficiently

abandoned. You ask how and I say:
cavern and ceiling and mind that is

home now to shaman and mystic—
where air flows into aperture,

and out of the darkness emerges
your own wild face.

The Lies that Save Us

Driving through Georgia,
we lie like Abraham.
Are you sisters? people ask.
Yes, we answer. *Twins, even.*
Though we are dressed similarly
in broad-brimmed hats,
long-sleeved shirts and tan pants
tucked into thick white socks
(it being tick season and all)—
we look nothing alike.
Thought so, people say,
as if they have figured out
some secret code. We smile back,
knowing the power of things unseen:
atoms, quarks, and auras,
and all the love that lies between.
Kissing energy, we call it.
But all they can see is
something.

This is Praying

This is Praying

For C., a resident at Riverbend Maximum Security Institution

I hear a voice speaking
about a bird dragging its dark universe
of feathers across our yard,

and I realize it must be me
telling the boy how I carried its body
beyond the range of our dogs.

One eye, round as a coin,
fixing fear upon me, the other,
half shut. How the bird hauled

its body back into our yard,
dying with a will I could only
admire. Telling the boy

just to tell him *something*.
I can barely see his face
through the slot, eight inches

from the bottom of the door.
Pie-hole, they call it. I know
he cannot be cured of his crime.

But I can't help myself—
this language my body speaks
as I crouch, palms, knees

pressed against the prison floor.
Am I the bird? the boy asks.
He is nineteen. He has an aunt,

a mother, both illiterate, both
a hundred miles away. No one knows why
they have stopped visiting.

I imagine his body, each Sunday,
learning again of their absence.
I imagine his organs, his bones

liquefying inside of his skin.
I imagine his eyes staring out
from his own gathered flesh.

It is three days before Christmas
and I have ten minutes to spread
something like joy. I think

of Vermeer, the woman in blue,
refusing to obey the physics
of light. I do not even know

the source of my own voice.
Am I the bird? There is a window
beyond the canvas but Vermeer

thinks a shadow will be
distracting. I tell him—the boy—
about a dream I'd had.

How my mind had been
like a living thing nailed down,
trembling with what ifs

and how comes. And then
these words: *I hear you,*
I hear you breathing. A sound

coming from within
and beyond. Not a voice, exactly.
More like a gentle pressing

of heat, the perfect distance
from flame, settling me immediately
into sleep. And now this voice

telling him I hear him,
I hear him breathing, telling him:
it is a beautiful sound.

Serving Time

For J., a resident at Riverbend Maximum Security Institution

Think fairy-fly, think
small wasp digging with her legs

through a water's skin.
Think wings, think fringed

and beautiful. Think
of the thing done

by a boy, that cannot be
undone. Think swim,

think down, think
of the paddles, which are really

wings, which are really
beautiful. And the thing done

by the boy that cannot be
undone. Think of the eggs

she is looking for: the eggs
of the water beetle into which

she will insert her own.
Think of the boy, think

of the thing done by the boy,
think of the boy undone

by a rage, undone
by its rising, rage undoing

what he thought he knew
of his mind, to undo that

of another. Think of the thing
done to a boy that cannot be

undone. Think of the eggs
which are not her eggs

which will become her own.
Wings, fringed

and beautiful. Think of her
exiting, think of her

climbing a stem—waterweed,
perhaps—without which

she would be unable
to lift her body

back into air. Think
of the boy, the beautiful boy.

Think of a thing done
that cannot be undone.

Mosaic of the Dark

Falling

Beyond the boundaries of wall and frame,
the rooms in which I live

pass holy into cell, sinew, and vein,
changing me with dark, abundant breath,

the way church bread changes some.
A rage at bombs and the odor of death,

or snow geese, lovely, coming out
from every page.

What Eye Is This

1. Twice Now I've Dreamed of Birds

What eye is this that rises
and falls, sudden flock
across a blue wake, billowing
as if body and sky
are one. As God becomes
the quarrel, becomes
confusion and descent,
fragment of exaltation. This
eye, this wisp of seeing
and being seen.

2. Omniscience, Prayer, Pantheon

A woman dreams of birds—
sudden flock across a blue wake—
as her god becomes
the quarrel, becomes
confusion and descent. She dreams
of atoms that won't be still,
of Lucretius, of pleasure,
and the nature of things. The sun's
green flash, the five notes
of a whippoorwill. She sings
about the eye that rises
and falls, billowing as if body
and sky are one. A woman
dreams of rain—knows
she was made for ruin—
its muscle sweet to her skin.

The History of Rain

The history of rain
is the history of hands,

gods in low hills
holding thunder

and flame. Rain pressed
into ash. The history of rain

is the history of prayer
(as syllable, as sound).

Small bones forced
into urns. The history of rain

is plague, is exile,
is horses and mud; sap

from tall trees, brewed
over fire. The history of rain

is male, is female; is burning
and being burned; hanging

and hanged. The history of rain
is the history of children

gnawing on roots;
the white of parched fields

lit by the moon.
The history of rain

is the history of semen
that softens the ground.

Is small and round
and perched on the shoulders

of a god's blue skin.
The history of rain

is the history of glass,
of vessels, ceramic and bronze,

silent as the bones
still waiting to rise.

This, Too, Is Praying

I love the darkness of a small town.
Graveyards I can walk by

and graveyards I can't.
I love femurs and old spears;

shards of small bowls rising up
from the earth's dry broth; the weight

of air on skin. I dream
of two black horses in a cave;

the eggs of arctic tern, hidden by stone;
of glaciers and uncountable bees.

I dream of flight. A sun
that can hold a million earths

and a mouth that swallows its fire.
Of the formless, watery waste thought

to be divine. I dream of atoms,
the gratuitous soul. Trance

of shaman, trance of child. Thinking
that presses the mind. Dear

god-shaped hole. Dear mountains
that can stop the rain. I dream

the beautiful going out
of flame.

Last Poem about My Mother

This is my mother
watching her heart—

dark, liquid motion
on the screen beside her.

How she called it
beautiful. This is

please and *thank you*,
and softens the wounds

of strangers. This is a body's
last words; what is left

after fire. This is cavities
in the bones of a bird

that make flight possible,
and flits unseen

through every gesture and word.
This is my mother

and a way out of my mother;
a place I can say

that I left.

Another Attempt at Praying

I've learned to love
the feel of stone

and to quiet my breath
when mourners come.

I dream of ancient paths
lined with trees

and the singing of gods;
the girl made of beads;

the deer in reds and blacks.
Footprints hardened

on a bank of sand say:
walk, pause, run.

I imagine their bodies
transformed into fish.

Into swallows. Fox lung
or beetle's blood.

A snake traveling through
dirt. Sometimes rain.

Who doesn't notice
the rain?

Even Houseflies

The day they entered our house
I did not know that their brains,

if separated from the body,
would resemble a single grain of sugar.

Or that liquid is their only intake,
requiring them to moisten anything solid

with their own saliva. Their lives,
an array of endless regurgitations.

And who's to say, after I'd killed
the last one—nine, maybe ten in all—

and resumed my reading,
only to be stopped by the words:

Even houseflies must have their angels
that it wasn't the angels themselves

who sent me to learn how they live.
Who's to say this wasn't the gesture

of some lively god pressing a small coin
into my heart. Like my mother

who won't stay dead, her eyes
fixing into mine like she knows

I'm her best chance. Like Ötzi
who keeps coming back—as shaman

or shepherd—in a cloak of woven grass;
the ease with which he walks

on hilly terrain. Or Pliny,
studious and brave, drawing a bath

too close to Pompeii. Who's to say
these aren't the gestures of gods. Active

during the day, but at night they rest
in the corners of rooms, where their eyes—

their thousands and thousands of eyes—
make a mosaic of the dark.

Notes

Matrimonies
"Sixth Grade": The name of the officiant in line 13 is not the
    boy's real name.

Testament
"Plumbing the Depths": *If God is male, then male is God* is
    from Mary Daly's *Beyond God the Father: Toward a
    Philosophy of Women's Liberation.*

Mosaic of the Dark
"Even Houseflies": The line *Even houseflies must have their
    angels* is from Rebecca Seiferle's poem "Seraphim."

Acknowledgments

Sincere gratitude to the editors of the following publications where these poems first appeared (unless otherwise noted), at times in earlier versions:

Bridges: A Jewish Feminist Journal: "The Lies that Save Us"
Broad Street: "Pretty Moon" (reprint)
CALYX: "Amanat"
Cave Wall: "Survival," "Sixth Grade," and "Induction"
Connotation Press: "Even Houseflies" and "Last Poem about My Mother"
Feminist Wire: "Commemoration" (reprint) and "Transaction"
Georgetown Review: "Clues"
The Greensboro Review: "Serving Time"
Journal of Feminist Studies in Religion: "Commemoration" and "On the Way to Emmaus"
New Millennium Writings: "Commemoration" (reprint)
N4728 Revue de poésie: "Plumbing the Depths"
Nimrod International Journal: "You Ask How," "Omniscience, Prayer, Pantheon," and "First Memory"
Poems & Plays: "Holy Week" and "Visitation"
Public Pool: "To Say Something Is Alive Is Not Enough," "Another Attempt at Praying," and "Elevator Ride with Famous Poet"
Rockhurst Review: "Proposal"
Rove Poetry: "Pretty Moon"
Sinister Wisdom: "Intersection" and "Recycling"
Sojourners: "This Is Praying"
Southern Women's Review: "Wedding"
The Sow's Ear Poetry Review: "Flash"
St. Sebastian Review: "Passing On"
StorySouth: "For the Cashier at T.R. Wolfe's Toy and Candy"

Tabula Rasa: Vanderbilt University Journal of Medical Humanities: "Holy Week" (reprint)
Vinyl Poetry: "The History of Rain"

Thanks to the editors of the following anthologies where these poems were reprinted, at times in earlier versions:

Forgotten Women (Grayson Books, 2017): "For the Cashier at T.R. Wolfe's Toy and Candy"
Nasty Women Poets: An Unapologetic Anthology of Subversive Verse (Lost Horse Press, 2017): "Plumbing the Depths"
New Poetry from the Midwest (New American Press, 2017): "Amanat," "Pretty Moon," and "This Is Praying"
Rainbow in the Word: LGBTQ Christians' Biblical Memoirs (Wipf and Stock, 2017): "The Lies that Save Us," "On the Way to Emmaus," and "Commemoration"
Best New Poets (University of Virginia Press, 2015): "Pretty Moon"
The Southern Poetry Anthology (Texas Review Press, 2013): "Wedding"
Milk and Honey (A Midsummer Night's Press, 2011): "The Lies that Save Us"

Thanks to Finishing Line Press for publishing *Commemoration*, in which the following poems appeared: "Commemoration," "Sixth Grade," "Survival," "Flash," "Wedding," "Recycling," "Intersection," "Holy Week," "Passing On," "Induction," "Clues," "On the Way to Emmaus," "Plumbing the Depths," and "The Lies that Save Us."

Endless thanks to Vanderbilt's MFA program, where many of these poems came into being, especially to Kate Daniels, Rick Hilles, and Mark Jarman.

To the following people for their guidance and inspiration at various points along the way: Emily August, Elizabeth Barnett, Destiny Birdsong, Alicia Brandewie, Kendra DeColo, the late Claudia Emerson, Keegan Finberg, Tanya Jarrett, Donika Kelly, Sarah Kersh, Susanna Kwan, Sarah Murphy, Stephanie Pruitt, Freya Sachs, and Christina Stoddard.

To my loving circle of family and friends for their enthusiasm and nurturing support.

To Diane Goettel for giving my work such a wonderful home.

And to Laurie. For everything.

Photo: Beth Gwinn

Lisa Dordal holds a Master of Divinity and a Master of Fine Arts, both from Vanderbilt University, and currently teaches in the English Department at Vanderbilt. She is a Pushcart Prize nominee and the recipient of the Robert Watson Literary Prize and an Academy of American Poets Prize. Her poetry has appeared in a variety of journals and anthologies including *Best New Poets, Ninth Letter, The Greensboro Review, Vinyl Poetry, CALYX, The Journal of Feminist Studies in Religion,* and *The Southern Poetry Anthology.* For more information, please visit her website: lisadordal.com.